# God's Road Map for Us

## The Plan of Holiness

FRANK MOORE

The *Holy Life* Bible Study Series

BOOK 1

Beacon Hill Press of Kansas City
Kansas City, Missouri

Copyright 2004
by Frank Moore and
Beacon Hill Press of Kansas City

ISBN 978-0-834-12109-6

Cover Design: Ted Ferguson

### Library of Congress Cataloging-in-Publication Data

Moore, Frank, 1951-
  God's road map for us : the plan of holiness / Frank Moore.
    p. cm. — (The holy life Bible study series ; bk. 1)
  ISBN 0-8341-2109-3 (pbk.)
  1. Holiness. 2. Holiness—Biblical teaching. I. Title II Series: Moore, Frank, 1951- . Holy life Bible study series ; bk. 1.

  BT767.M674 2004
  248.4'071—dc22

                          2004003067

10 9 8 7 6 5 4 3 2

# Contents

## CONTENTS

# For the Group Leader

## How to Use This Study Book

We trust that this study will be a valuable resource to you and others in helping you grow in holiness and Christlikeness. It is written and organized to be used as a small-group Bible study, with 12 weekly sessions. The following are some brief guidelines to help you maximize your group's time together.

1. Pray regularly throughout the week that your group sessions will be times of warm fellowship and genuine spiritual growth. Most of all, ask that the Holy Spirit will be present in a powerful way, speaking to and challenging each group member to a life of holiness. Open and close each weekly session in prayer.
2. Prepare well for each session. Carefully study the scripture readings and exposition prior to your group meeting, which will help you facilitate the discussions and keep them moving.
3. Use the group discussion questions and activities to promote lively dialog among group members. Feel free to contribute your own comments as well, but don't allow any one member of the group (including yourself) to dominate the discussions.
4. Whenever it's practical, link your own comments to those of others. Affirm each group member. This will help encourage some of the more reticent members of your group to participate in the discussions.
5. Respect the confidentiality of what is shared within the group.
6. Encourage group members to come to each session prepared, having studied the lesson and scriptures carefully, in addition to having meditated on the personal reflection questions.
7. Encourage any group member who has made any type of personal decision for Christ (salvation, sanctification, or

other) to make his or her decision public as soon as possible at one of your church's worship services.

# Welcome to the Adventure

**Col. 1:9-22**

If you're using this book as part of a group Bible study, take a few minutes to go around the room and have each participant tell something about himself or herself. If class members don't already know each other, have each one share a fact that gives insight into his or her personality or interests. If class members already know each other pretty well, have them share something about themselves that's not widely known. This will open the way for better discussion of the Bible later.

The wonder and amazement of a child generates excitement wherever it's manifest. Isn't it exciting to see a child's face light up the first time he or she plays with a puppy or blows a big bubble with bubble gum or jumps into the deep end of the swimming pool? How about a young teenager's excitement the first time he or she rides the biggest, worst roller coaster in the state? How about an older teen's thrill of taking the family car out for the first time? That hunger for wonder and amazement carries over into adulthood as grown-ups participate in the "extreme sports" craze. I don't know about you, but some of those extreme sporting events look downright dangerous to me! My life is exciting enough without jumping off of a bridge with a bungee cord tied to my leg or sailing down a snowy mountain trail on a snowboard!

What is it with our fascination with new experiences or big adventures? It appears that God hardwires an adventuresome spirit into most of us. I say "most of us" because I have a few friends who seem content to sit on porch swings and watch the grass grow. They're not the norm, though. We seem to come into the world with a human nature that compels us to seek out new experiences. We love to explore and try new things. Add a little danger or some risk to the mix, and we're *really* fired up!

I had my own share of childhood adventures. I grew up on a farm with one sister and two brothers. We didn't have neighbors with children our age—we barely had neighbors—so we played with each other. We didn't have the full range of toys that youngsters have today, but we created our own games and pastimes with the objects we found around the farm. Bikes, boards, and ropes took on fresh possibilities when we got our hands on them. We all had pretty active imaginations that kept us exploring in the woods and fields. We also liked to take things apart to see how they worked. More than once our mother scolded us for disassembling our toys to analyze the secret of their operation. One thing remained certain—we were never bored!

My childhood memories remind me of humanity's natural inclination for exciting adventures. Some folks, like me, carry a natural curiosity into each and every day—a curiosity that causes us to take things apart to analyze their function. I don't know why, but God just made us this way. I'm glad He did, though. Curiosity gives added value to life.

## PERSONAL REFLECTION

Think about your own childhood.

1. What were some of your childhood adventures?


2. What things feed your curiosity?


3. Where did your early explorations in life take you?

This book offers you an adventurous journey. It will appeal to your curiosity as you take biblical stories and concepts apart to gain a better understanding of them. It will lay out a road map for you as you set out on an amazing journey with God and He works with each of us through the highs and lows of this thing called life. God's experience with parenting us is nothing short of an extreme sport—for Him *and* for us! Words fail to adequately describe the strain on His patience and nerves as He walks beside us and parents us through our lives. By studying the adventure story of Bible characters on their journeys with God, we'll gain new insights into God's dealings with us today. By dissecting and exploring the admonitions of Scripture, we'll discover new facets of God's hopes and dreams for our lives.

## GROUP DISCUSSION

Take a few minutes to give the members of your group a chance to formulate their responses to the following questions. Then share everyone's answers with the group.

1. Relate a time in your life when God revealed a new truth to you or gave you a new spiritual insight.

2. How did God reveal this new truth or insight to you?

3. How has the Bible figured into your spiritual growth and development?

4. In what ways might parenting compare with "extreme sports"?

5. How might our experiences with parenting our children compare to God's experience with parenting us?

## READ COL. 1:9-22

We won't explore Col. 1:9-22 in depth at this time. Nor will we discuss the richness of its meaning. We begin this book by looking at this passage as a signpost that points out the direction our journey will take us in the weeks ahead. Note briefly the following things about these verses. Feel free as time permits to discuss further with class members any of these general observations:

1. God wants to fill us with knowledge and understanding of His will (v. 9).
2. God wants us to live lives worthy of our Creator (v. 10).
3. God wants us to live lives that please Him in every way (v. 10).
4. God wants our lives to bear the fruit of good works (v. 10).
5. God wants us to grow in our knowledge of Him (v. 10).
6. God wants to strengthen us with His power (v. 11).
7. God wants to give us endurance and patience (v. 11).
8. We should give thanks to God for all He does to make us saints in His kingdom (v. 12).
9. We have been rescued from darkness and brought into spiritual light (v. 13).
10. Christ brings us redemption through the forgiveness of our sins (v. 14).
11. Christ is the best picture we have of our Heavenly Father (vv. 15-19).
12. Our redemption comes through Christ's blood shed on the Cross (v. 20).

13. We were once alienated from God because of our sins (v. 21).
14. One of God's purposes in working with us is to make us holy (v. 22).

## GROUP DISCUSSION

1. What catches your eye in Col. 1:9-22?

2. What amazes you most about God's plan of salvation for us?

3. Do God's desires and dreams for us seem realistic? Why or why not?

4. In which of these ways do you see God already working in your life?

5. In which of these ways could you use a boost in your life?

This Bible study is going to provide you with new insights about Scripture, yourself, and God's plan for your life. It's going to stretch you, take you outside your comfort zone at times, and force you to think in new ways about spiritual matters. This study may occasionally give you the feeling of jumping from an airplane, hopefully with a well-packed parachute. Your mind may free-fall through many new ideas as you discover new insights regarding God's incredible plan of salvation. You're certainly going to feel the puzzle of unanswered questions from time to time. And occasionally you're going to feel like a three-year-old asking "Why?" at every turn of the page.

All this questioning and discovery is OK, because you're on a big adventure. God planted that exploration bug in you. He loves it when you let your spiritual imagination take you into unexplored territory to discover new insights about yourself, your salvation, and your God.

So welcome to the journey! It's going to be exciting, and we're going to have some fun along the way. Just pretend with me for a while that you're a kid again. Read the Bible and study it with your friends as if you were reading it for the very first time. You'll be amazed at all God says to you and at His incredible plan of salvation for you.

## GROUP ACTIVITY

Close your time together with a prayer that God will bless your efforts and thrill your hearts over and over again with knowledge and understanding of His Word and its application to your lives. Ask Him to help each of you make the most of this study about your adventure with Him.

## FURTHER QUESTIONS

Take a moment at the conclusion of the session to encourage class participants to place their unanswered questions on note cards, along with this session number. They should then place their cards in an "odds and ends" box provided by the Bible study leader. Attention will be given to these questions in the last session of this study.

# Meeting God

Exod. 3:1-6; Isa. 6:1-7

If we want to fully understand a good book, we must know something about its author. Historical sites along the highway mean more to us if we know something about the people who made the history. A beautiful song carries a deeper meaning if we know the person it was written for or about. Life's like that—it's more about people than events or objects. So just about every one of life's searches for new understanding will put us on a road that leads us to study and learn about individuals in one way or another.

## GROUP DISCUSSION

1. How does knowing about people, who they are, and what they're like contribute to our understanding of a good book, a beautiful song, or a historical site?

2. Describe your best friend. What characteristics about this person help you paint a colorful picture for your description?

Learning about individuals is also important when it comes to understanding our religious faith. If we want to know what we believe and why, we must know certain truths about God. Our faith should never be composed of a set of sacred ideas that we memorize and recite like a preschooler reciting the alphabet. Our faith is about our relationship with a living Being, and it's vital that we get to know Him, our

Creator and Father, better. As we do, we get a new grip on what we believe and why we believe it. So let's begin this Bible study by pursuing a journey with God.

## GROUP ACTIVITY

Divide the class in half. Have group 1 answer questions 1 and 3 (below). Have group 2 answer questions 2 and 3. Have each group share its answers when ready.

1. In your own words, describe who God *is.*

2. What words characterize what God is *like?*

3. What makes you think these things? In other words, where is your evidence?

The Bible tells us about God through stories of everyday people in everyday situations—people like you and me. We tend to think Bible characters participated in big adventures every day of their lives. But that's not the way it was. Most of their days were just as ordinary as most of our days. Right in the middle of all that routine, God popped into their lives from time to time. Every time He did, He taught something about himself. In this week's Bible study, we're going to look at a couple of men in the Bible who encountered God. Let's see what we learn about our Creator and Father from these encounters.

GROUP DISCUSSION

Think of a recent event at your house in which you learned a lesson about people or human nature through the way they behaved.

READ EXOD. 3:1-6

Life doesn't get any more ordinary than leading a flock of sheep across a hot, barren desert. And you thought *your* life was boring! Right in the middle of this rather mundane activity, God appeared to Moses. And here we learn important lessons about God.

1. How did Moses end up out in the middle of the desert, exiled from his family and friends?

2. Do you think Moses was actively seeking a visual audience with God that day, or do you think God initiated this encounter?

3. Why did this particular bush catch Moses' attention?

4. How does God usually get your attention?

5. Why do you think God often portrayed himself as fire in the Bible? What properties of fire give us clues into what God is like?

6. Why did God tell Moses not to come closer as he approached the burning bush?

7. Why did God tell Moses to take off his sandals?

God often speaks through understatements. Take the burning bush in this story (Exod. 3:1-6) for example. God could have put on a fireworks show for Moses, complete with lightning and fireballs darting across the sky, which would have made a Fourth of July celebration look like a fizzling wet match in comparison. But He didn't. God chose to work through an ordinary piece of scrub brush.

What was the object lesson for Moses that day? God is holy. Moses responded to this encounter with God with respect, humility, and worship. So should we. Moses had several other encounters with God throughout his lifetime. In this particularly dramatic one, God began with Truth Number One: God is holy.

### READ ISA. 6:1-7

Isa. 6:1-7 finds Isaiah, a godly minister, disillusioned and discouraged. His hero and friend, King Uzziah, had just died. The nation was thrown into leadership transition. Isaiah went through the motions of leading a worship service at the Temple. Then something special happened. God intervened. What Isaiah experienced that day changed his life forever.

## GROUP DISCUSSION

1. What broke Isaiah's downcast mood that day?

2. What overwhelmed Isaiah with this vision?

3. What was the message of the song God's attendants sang?

4. What is the symbolism of the fire in this vision?

5. What is the fire to accomplish in Isaiah?

6. What do you learn about God from Isaiah's vision?

7. What does this understanding of God mean to your life?

Both Moses and Isaiah found themselves caught up in the routine of ordinary life. Both experienced a personal encounter with the living God. Both learned that first and foremost, God wanted them to grasp the fact that He is holy.

## GROUP DISCUSSION

1. Why do you suppose this fundamental truth, that God is holy, is so important to our understanding of Him?

2. Why do you suppose God wants to make sure that we grasp this truth?

3. How might we live if we served an unholy God?

4. How, then, should we live since we serve a holy God?

## FOR FURTHER STUDY

God's holiness is frequently described or emphasized in the Bible. Look at the passages below and note what they tell us about God.

Exod. 15:11—

1 Sam. 6:20—

Ps. 99:9—

Rev. 15:4—

List other biblical passages that point us in the direction of God's holiness.

1.

2.

3.

## FURTHER QUESTIONS

Take a moment at the conclusion of the session to encourage class participants to place their unanswered questions on note cards, along with this session number. They should then place their cards in an "odds and ends" box provided by the Bible study leader. Attention will be given to these questions in the last session of this study.

# In His Image

**Gen. 1:27-28, 31; 5:1**

A special speaker at our church recently gave a humorous presentation of photographs showing how dogs of various breeds resemble their owners. These dogs and their owners had faces, noses, hairstyles, and other features that made them look alike. While that may seem absurd for animals and their owners, we know that many children really do favor their parents in a variety of ways. We've seen it so often that we've come to expect it.

## GROUP DISCUSSION

1. Give examples of families you know in which children resemble their parents.

2. What personality characteristics do children often adopt from their parents?

The Bible tells us that humanity was created in God's image. Incredible thought! We favor God in a variety of ways. Our ability to self-reflect, to plan for our future, plus our spiritual nature, our higher communication skills, our creative ability, and our never-dying souls all remind us of the divine image we bear. God is the most awesome Being in all of reality. He defines perfection in every way. Yet He chose to share a part of himself by creating humanity in His image.

1. Gen. 1:27 is the first poem in the Bible. What is the significance of the word "created" being used three times in such a short verse?

2. Do these passages of scripture seem to indicate that God was actively involved in bringing humanity into existence, or did He stand idly by and watch it evolve on its own?

3. What is the significance of God's placing of a blessing on humanity?

4. How did God feel about His creation of humanity?

5. Why did God wait until the last day of creation to place humanity on the scene?

One can't read this biblical material without realizing how much planning and thought God placed in His creative work. As He neared the end of the initial creative activity described in Gen. 1, He placed humanity in the midst of the picture. Humanity became the highest and noblest of God's creative activity. Like placing a cherry on top of an ice cream dessert, God saved the best for last!

## PERSONAL REFLECTION

1. How does it make you feel to be reminded that you were purposefully created by God?

2. What does this say to us about the way we should treat each other?

3. Do these Bible verses help you realize that you belong to God?

4. What does belonging to God mean to you?

5. How might that awareness affect the way you live?

A central theme of this material reminds us that humanity bears the image of God. That means we resemble Him in a variety of ways. How? This concept seems difficult to get our minds around until we think reflectively about it. See if this question helps frame it for you. How do you differ from your pet (or any other member of the animal kingdom)?

## GROUP DISCUSSION

1. Think of ways in which you differ from your pet.

2. The biblical text shows God's reasoning ability. How does your ability to reason differ from that of your pet?

3. The biblical text pictures God as a social being who has a desire to interact with His creatures. What capacities do we have for interacting with one another?

4. The biblical text demonstrates God's creative ability. How is our creative ability like God's creative ability? How is God's creative ability different from ours?

5. The biblical text describes God as charging humanity with the responsibility of caring for His creation. How do we do this?

6. The Bible often refers to God as a Spirit. How is our spirit like God's Spirit?

It does us good from time to time to go back and study our heritage. We do this when we look through old photo albums, attend family reunions, or look through a keepsake drawer in the bedroom dresser. These verses of scripture give us an opportunity to go back and review our roots. Like baby pictures in an old family album, the Bible reminds us that we didn't just happen on the scene. We were carefully planned for, crafted, and lovingly placed in the center of all God had labored to create.

I used to know a girl with low self-esteem who had a favorite saying she recited to herself when she felt particularly low. She would stand up tall in front of the mirror, square her shoulders, and shout in a loud voice, "I *am* somebody!" Her declaration reminded her and announced to the world that she was not the worm she felt like. It forced her to rethink her view of herself and her circumstances.

## PERSONAL REFLECTION

Read Gen. 1:27-28, 31 and 5:1 again, and then answer these questions:

1. How should you feel about yourself in light of these verses?

2. What do you think God wants you to believe about Him after reading these verses?

3. If you really are made in the image of God, how should you then live?

## FOR FURTHER STUDY

Job 32:8

1 Pet. 1:18-19

John 3:16

## FURTHER QUESTIONS

Take a moment at the conclusion of the session to encourage class participants to place their unanswered questions on note cards, along with this session number. They should then place their cards in an "odds and ends" box provided by the Bible study leader. Attention will be given to these questions in the last session of this study.

# Created to Be Holy

**Exod. 19:6; Lev. 11:44-45; 19:2; Eph. 1:4; 1 Pet. 2:9**

Think of God's dealings with the Hebrew people in the Old Testament—from Genesis to Malachi—as one big object lesson. It's much easier for us to see the big picture from farther down the road of time than it was for them as they lived the biblical events. In our previous study we saw how God created us in His image. Now let's look at God's desires for us as we live our daily lives.

The first few chapters of Genesis tell us about the early days of humanity on the earth. The story quickly focuses on one man, Abraham, and the nation that sprung up from his descendents. After settling in the land that God promised Abraham, these offspring moved to Egypt and spent 400 years as aliens and slaves. God delivered them through the efforts of Moses and brought them back to the Promised Land. As they wandered from Egypt back to Israel for 40 years, God talked to Moses about His plans for His people.

## GROUP DISCUSSION

1. If you're a parent, did you have parental hopes and dreams for your children when they were born? What were they? If you're not a parent, what were your parents' hopes and dreams for you when you were born?

2. Do you think God had parental hopes and dreams for humanity when He created us?

3. What might some of God's hopes and dreams for us have been?


## READ EXOD. 19:6

In Exod. 19:6 we see some of the hopes and dreams God had for His people. Exod. 19:6 tells us that God wants to make us into "a kingdom of priests and a holy nation." The Israelites were to be God's kingdom and recognize God as their King. They were to think of themselves as His representatives on earth, wholly consecrated to Him and dedicated to His service. Similar thoughts regarding this spiritual relationship with God are found in Isa. 61:6; 1 Pet. 2:5; Rev. 1:6; and Rev. 5:10. Take a moment to read each of these verses and note how, from beginning to end, the Bible portrays this same image of a kingdom of priests and a holy nation.


## GROUP ACTIVITY

Give every class participant a note card. Ask half of the class to write their answers to question 1 (below) on the card. Ask the other half of the class to write their answers to question 2. The leader should collect all cards and read them aloud.

1. What plans or goals do you think God had in mind for His people when He referred to them as a "kingdom of priests" and "a holy nation"?


2. God's people are to set themselves apart for relationship and life with Him. What does that imply about the way we're to conduct ourselves in daily living?

## READ 1 PET. 2:9 AND EPH. 1:4

Peter expanded this same thought a bit in 1 Peter 2:9 when He referred to God's people as "a chosen people, a royal priesthood, a holy nation, a people belonging to God." Paul expressed the same thought in Eph. 1:4 when he said God planned for us to be "holy and blameless in his sight."

## PERSONAL REFLECTION

1. The Bible says that you're chosen, royal, holy, and belong to God. Explore your thoughts on what God has in mind for your life.

2. What does "holy and blameless" look like in God's plan for you?

3. What needs to change in your life for His plan to become or remain a reality?

Sometimes parents set the expectation bar for their children's accomplishments so high that it's realistically impossible to attain. The grades are never quite good enough; the wins at the ballpark are too few; the mastery of the musical instrument falls short of the goal. God, however, never does that to His children. The dreams and goals He has for us are all realistic and realizable—that is, with His direction, strength, and assistance. So bear in mind as you work through this Bible study that God is not tying a carrot to a stick and holding it just out of your reach as an unrealistic goal. Satan would like for us to write off God's dream as unattainable. Don't listen to him. It's another one of his lies.

READ LEV. 11:44-45; 19:2

Leviticus is often referred to as the Book of Holiness. It uses the word "holy" more than any other book in the Bible, and it gives more specific examples of what is and is not holy than any other biblical book. We noted in Study 1 that God is a holy God. The Bible is filled with references supporting this. Study 2 reminded us that we were created in His image. It's quite reasonable, then, that in this study we hear God telling us to be holy because He is holy. God wanted His people to set themselves apart from all the other nations of the world and exercise total allegiance to Him. That meant that their lives would be lived differently than their neighbors' lives.

Sounds overwhelming, doesn't it? How could we possibly be holy as God is holy? It looks as though God has set the bar pretty high! But don't despair. He hints at how it's possible and what He has in mind in Lev. 11:45—"I am the LORD who brought you up out of Egypt to be your God."

God reminds the Israelites more than 60 times in the Old Testament that He delivered them from Egypt. Recount all God did for His people during the trip from Egypt to the Promised Land: Red Sea deliverance, manna delivered daily, fresh water in the desert, a guiding cloud by day and a protecting fire by night. The list of all the things God did for His people during that trip is long. In no way could one read those stories and think the Israelites pulled the deliverance off all by themselves. From departure day until they arrived at the finish line, God worked for them and with them. They reached the goal only because He helped them reach it.

## GROUP DISCUSSION

1. What does God's deliverance from Egypt for Israel say about His ability to help you with your life?

2. Can you live a holy life by yourself?

3. Why or why not?

4. What do you seem to be lacking: will power, information, endurance, or something else?

## PERSONAL REFLECTION

How will God have to help you if you're to be the person He's dreamed and planned for you to be?

## FOR FURTHER STUDY

The Father's dreams and plans for us are presented in various places throughout the Bible. Look at the following passages for further insight into God's plan for us to be His special people:

Isa. 44:1-5

Isa. 61:6-7

1 Pet. 2:4-6

List other biblical passages that indicate God's plan for His people.

1.

2.

3.

## FURTHER QUESTIONS

Take a moment at the conclusion of the session to encourage class participants to place their unanswered questions on note cards, along with this session number. They should then place their cards in an "odds and ends" box provided by the Bible study leader. Attention will be given to these questions in the last session of this study.

# The Way We Were

**Gen. 1:27—2:25**

History is fascinating to me. Whether standing in Jamestown, Virginia, and imagining the original settlers arriving, or standing on the battlefield in Gettysburg, Pennsylvania, and imagining the guns firing from the hillsides, I love to visit locations with historical significance and recreate the era in my mind. The exercise gets me in touch with the past and teaches me important lessons about life.

It's good for us to occasionally revisit the Garden of Eden in our minds and recount what God originally had in mind for humanity and His world. It helps us to remember the way we had it once upon a time and the way God intended things to be for us on this earth. Our purpose in this mental exercise is not so we can feel sorry for ourselves for losing paradise. Rather, we want to gain a sense of direction for the way God wants to bring us back to himself.

## GROUP DISCUSSION

1. What historical sights have you visited in your lifetime?

2. What lessons did you learn from these visits?

## READ GEN. 1:26-31

Gen. 1:26-31 contains the first use of poetry in the Bible. God's creative work is emphasized three times in verse 27 as a reminder that humanity and everything else on this earth did not spring to life by chance. Everything on earth arrived here crafted and delivered from the hand of God. God placed us in a perfect environment. He provided a perfectly balanced plant and animal kingdom. The land, sea, and atmosphere provided everything necessary for enjoying life to its fullest potential. The beauty in design and color were breathtaking; the flowers and trees excited the senses of sight, smell, and touch. The fruit of the trees dripped with rich flavor. God anticipated every human need and thought of every detail.

## PERSONAL REFLECTION

Does God's attention to every detail of creation help you see just how special you are to Him? Take a moment and thank your loving Heavenly Father for planning and caring so well for you.

During times of fanciful dreaming we all ponder the thought of how much better our lives would be if we just had more cooperative circumstances. If the weather weren't so hot or so cold, if the work were more enjoyable, if the living environment were somehow more conducive, then we would really be living. This passage of scripture reminds us that our dreams of a more ideal world would not necessarily satisfy us. Adam and Eve had the best of all possible environments, but it wasn't enough for them. They quested for something more.

## GROUP DISCUSSION

1. If you could change some things about your current situation in life, what would they be?

2. Now be honest with yourself: would these changes really satisfy you, or would you then long for something else?

3. Why is it that we never seem to be satisfied with our current set of circumstances no matter how good they are? Or why is it we don't seem to know what we have until we lose it?

Notice in this passage that Adam and Eve had both the privilege of a perfect environment and a responsibility to care for God's created order. So they had a purpose to occupy their time and all the necessary resources to fulfill their responsibilities. God granted the couple the authority to rule over everything in the earth and to enjoy the bounty it provided. He pronounced a blessing on the couple and all He had made. He said it was "very good." Thus, God gave himself an A+ for a job well done. No words adequately describe the feelings that wash over a craftsman when he or she stands back and looks at the finished product of carefully crafted handiwork—a piece of furniture, a piece of pottery, a craft object. That finished product speaks volumes of satisfaction to its creator. That's just a fraction of what God must have felt as He cast a wide-angle look at all He had made.

## PERSONAL REFLECTION

Think of the feeling you experienced the last time your creative ability helped you produce an item from a craft, construction, or art project. How might God's feelings at the end of the sixth day of creation be mirrored in your feelings?

Remember—it wasn't as if Adam and Eve didn't have anything to do. Actually they had plenty to keep them occupied. God commissioned them to colonize the earth. Their agricultural responsibilities to cultivate their food, their geographic responsibilities to explore and map uncharted lands, their scientific responsibilities to discover God's hidden laws of nature, and their mechanical responsibilities to use their sharp minds to think up inventions provided enough challenge to keep them busy for a lifetime. We sometimes think our lives would be perfect if we could divest ourselves of all responsibility and do nothing. We see in this passage that even in the most ideal setting on the earth, the first couple did not lack things to do. Idle hands or an idle mind for long periods of time can become dangerous.

## GROUP ACTIVITY

Divide the class into three groups, and assign one of the three questions below to each group. After group members have discussed their responses, have each group report to the entire class.
1. Why did God design life on earth for us to be filled with activity?

2. In what ways is responsibility the flip side of privilege?

3. Give examples from home, school, church, or work of how privilege and responsibility go hand in hand.

READ GEN. 2:1-25

Gen. 2:1-25 is the same story told from a little different vantage point as Gen. 1. This time the emphasis shifts from the created order to the first couple and from a distant creator God to an intimate, personal God. The name "Eden" (v. 8) means paradise or bliss. Again, God attended to every detail in this ideal world. Mention of the two trees in verse 9 reminds us that Adam and Eve had these objects as constant reminders that life itself came their way as a gift from God and that as His creatures they had moral responsibility to default to His wisdom regarding matters of good and evil. They were free to eat the fruit from the tree of life but not from the tree of the knowledge of good and evil.

The emphasis in the story is not on the one thing the pair could *not* do but on the million-and-one things they *could* do. They even were given permission to eat from God's special tree of life. We don't know for sure, but it appears that this symbolizes eternal life for Adam and Eve as long as they followed God's directions for them. God gave both of them a conscience that directed them to do what He asked and to avoid what was forbidden. The tree of knowledge of good and evil gave them a visual reminder of what they knew in their hearts.

Picture it like this: God gave Adam and Eve a book of "dos" and "don'ts." The "do" chapter gave them permission to participate in thousands of activities; the "don't" chapter had one prohibition in it. God asked only that they not seek to be morally independent from Him. In other words, they should let Him define right and wrong for them.

## GROUP DISCUSSION

1. Why do you think God created a visual reminder of humanity's dependence on Him for life?

2. Why did God create a visual reminder of their need to allow Him to define right and wrong for them?

3. Why is it so hard for us humans to let God set the moral boundaries for us and tell us what's right and wrong?

Freedom is a two-way street. So is free will. Both allow us to do some things while forbidding us from doing others. You can't have a free will that works only when you choose to make right decisions any more than you can have water that will quench your thirst without the potential to drown you. So Gen. 2:16-17 reminds us that even in a perfect environment, the innocent couple was on probation just as we find ourselves today. We sometimes think, *If I didn't have to deal with temptation and moral choices, life would be perfect.* No it wouldn't; it wouldn't be human life as God created it. Adam and Eve had the perfect life, but they also had the responsibility of defaulting to God for His definitions of right and wrong. That proved to be a tougher responsibility than the first couple ever thought possible.

## GROUP DISCUSSION

1. Why must freedom or free will logically be a two-way street?

2. What responsibilities come with the gift of free will?

3. Living on probation sometimes seems like a risky thing. How can we minimize our risk when it comes to making moral choices as God intends?

Ah—we see here the Golden Age of Innocence. Nakedness symbolized a freedom from shame. God created the first couple with both incredible privilege and incredible responsibility. He also created them with moral innocence. They knew nothing other than to believe, trust, and follow God—much like a three-year-old child looks to his or her parents for direction and protection. God provided everything the couple could ever need physically or spiritually. Moral innocence sounds virtuous, but it's not truly virtuous until it's tried, just as our infatuation with another person isn't true love until it passes a battery of tests. In other words, this visit to the original home of our original parents reminds us that even in paradise a resolve and conviction to follow God had to be tested. The same is true for us today. It's one thing to say, "I love God." It's quite another to prove it by depending on Him daily for both life and moral conviction.

## PERSONAL REFLECTION

1. How would your life be different if you had never known guilt or shame, and if you had no scars from past sins?

2. Why must our moral innocence be tried or tested in life?

3. How do you prove your love for God in your daily life?

## FOR FURTHER STUDY

Ps. 8:1-9

Gen. 9:2

Ps. 139:13-17

## FURTHER QUESTIONS

Take a moment at the conclusion of the session to encourage class participants to place their unanswered questions on note cards, along with this session number. They should then place their cards in an "odds and ends" box provided by the Bible study leader. Attention will be given to these questions in the last session of this study.

## Choosing Not to Follow Directions

**Gen. 3:1-13**

I grew up on a farm. When I was a child I spent a lot of my time hoeing in the fields, and as I teenager I drove the tractor. I remember a day from my childhood when my dad took me to the cornfield and left me with specific directions on how to chop the weeds from around the young stalks. I thought I understood his instructions, and he left me there with both of us confident that I knew what to do. But when he came to check on me a couple of hours later, healthy weeds were blowing in the breeze, and the young cornstalks were chopped and dying in the middle of the rows.

God may have felt like my dad the day He gave Adam and Eve His plan for their lives in the Garden of Eden. The plan was amazingly simple—enjoy yourselves in paradise, do what you want to do, eat what you want to eat, stay away from the fruit of only one tree. God gave them a great deal of privilege and asked them to assume very little responsibility. When He checked on them later, however, He discovered that His children had chosen not to follow His simple directions.

### GROUP DISCUSSION

1. How was my (the author's) failure to follow my father's plan like Adam and Eve's failure to follow their Father's plan?

2. What is the pivotal difference between my failure and the first couple's failure as it relates to intention and desire?

3. Did Adam and Eve understand what God asked of them? Do you think God's instructions to them were presented in a clear, understandable manner?

READ GEN. 3:1-13

Let's analyze the details of the account found in Gen. 3:1-13. All sorts of insights are hidden within the details. First, note that the serpent was crafty and shrewd. He was an analytical thinker and a smooth talker. Always remember: the tempter's voice in your ear is *carefully reasoned* and *seductively persuasive.* Next, observe that the serpent is a creature, not a god. The serpent held no power over God and had only the power of suggestion over Adam and Eve. Think about it; your tempter can only *suggest* sinful options. He can't make you sin. Notice in Gen. 3:1 how the serpent misquoted God. In so doing, God's character and proper provision for His children were called into question. The tempter implied that since God had not properly provided for Adam and Eve, their only choice was to take matters into their own hands and provide for themselves.

GROUP ACTIVITY

1. How does the tempter's misquoting of God's command call His character into question?

2. How does the tempter's misquoting of God's command imply that He is either mean or unconcerned about Adam and Eve's needs?

3. Compare God's command in Gen. 2:17 with Eve's quotation of that command in Gen. 3:2-3. What did she add to God's command that He did not say?

4. How did the tempter and Eve both distort the facts about God?

5. According to Gen. 3:4-5, what role does doubt play in breaking down our resistance to temptation?

6. The serpent was correct in that the couple did not physically die that day. However, their actions broke fellowship with their God. What died that day?

The serpent reserved his best weapon of logic for last. The punch line of the argument promises the couple the opposite of what God warned against. Rather than dying, disobedience to God's command would give them everything they had ever hoped for. Again, the implication of this argument suggested that God was withholding good things from the couple. According to the tempter, they needed to recognize what was best for them and act accordingly, even if it meant choosing not to follow God directions. In essence, the crown jewel of all suggestions to our first parents sounded something like this: "Only *you* know what's best for you. You must take matters into your own hands and decide for yourself what's right and wrong for you. No one can determine that but you."

## PERSONAL REFLECTION

The serpent's crown jewel argument gets top billing in today's culture. How does society or your friends appeal to you to take matters into your own hands and decide for yourself what's right and wrong for you? In what ways are you told daily, "No one can determine what's best for you but you"?

Temptation always appeals to us on several levels. Take for example the allure of a new car. It looks, sounds, and smells great; it meets your practical need for reliable transportation; it has all of the power and features you'll need for road trips. The first couple's temptation appealed to their physical need for food; the forbidden fruit appealed to their aesthetic appreciation of beauty; the suggestion appealed to their intellectual desire for wisdom. The tempter cast a lure with several hooks in it. Like a skilled fisherman, he baited the hooks and reeled Eve in. Adam appears to have followed suit without resistance. He didn't even bother to question his mate's suggestion. He chose obedience to his mate over obedience to his God. Adam and Eve represented humanity badly that day, and we've all followed their example in our own lives since that day.

## GROUP DISCUSSION

1. Why were the serpent's tempting suggestions so appealing?

2. In what ways does the tempter use these same arguments on us today?

3. Why do you suppose Adam offered no resistance to his mate's suggestion to join her in disobedience?

4. Why did neither of them suggest they discuss this matter with God before making a decision?

5. How did their disobedience alienate them from God and from one another?

6. How did they respond to their alienation from one another? (3:7).

7. How did they respond to their alienation from God? (3:8).

When the time arrived for their afternoon walk, all-knowing God called out for the couple the way we call for our small children when they're playing a game of hide-and-seek with us. Of course, He knew where they were. He patiently preferred to draw them out rather than embarrass them with a startling exposure. He could have focused a bright beam of light right on them and shouted, "Gotcha!" But He didn't. He could have said, "Thought you could hide from My all-seeing eyes, huh?" But He didn't. God's personality often manifests itself in understatement and patience.

Once they presented themselves to Him, accountability for their actions followed. God always draws rather than drives us to himself. We, too, must accept accountability for our disobedient actions. Just as the serpent led the first couple astray with questions, so God drew them back to himself with questions (to which He already knew the answers). Again, He used parental patience in helping His children come to terms with their failure.

## GROUP DISCUSSION

1. Why did God question the couple rather than accuse them?

2. Why did Adam and Eve both play the game of "Blame Someone Else"?

3. How are we sometimes like them in playing the blame game when it comes to taking responsibility for our actions?

## FOR FURTHER STUDY

The Bible presents us with the truths of this week's passage in other passages. Check these additional scriptures regarding sin. What new insights do you learn from them?

Rom. 8:7

James 1:14-15

Ps. 51:3-5

## FURTHER QUESTIONS

Take a moment at the conclusion of the session to encourage class participants to place their unanswered questions on note cards, along with this session number. They should then place their cards in an "odds and ends" box provided by the Bible study leader. Attention will be given to these questions in the last session of this study.

# Restoration Promised

**Gen. 3:14-19**

*Trouble Hits Paradise. Eden Not Perfect After All.* That's how the headlines of the *Eden News* might have read the next morning. God's plan was almost derailed that day. Talk about a train wreck! As powerful as He was, God didn't turn the hands on the clock back and undo the decisions of His children or the consequences of their bad choices. He didn't have a way within His sovereign plan for His children to unlearn their carnal knowledge; neither do we. One of the toughest experiences a parent faces is sitting down with a child and helping him or her regroup after an act of sin or disobedience has put him or her in contact with sights or information the parent hoped the child would never encounter. The inability to undo the past is a helpless feeling. Carnal knowledge tattoos a dark image on our souls with nearly permanent ink.

## PERSONAL REFLECTION

If you're a parent, recall a time in your parenting experience when you assisted your child through coming to terms with a sin or act of disobedience. If you're not a parent, recall a time when you had to come to terms with a sin or act of disobedience either in your life or the life of a friend.

It was totally within God's ability to snap His finger that day and wipe the slate clean, ending the experiment right then and there—the experiment of giving free will to creatures. But He didn't. Like any loving parent, He sat down with them, right in the middle of the mess His children had made of their lives. He talked them through it. Read the text again. Not once did He say, "I told you so," or "Why didn't you just listen to me?" or "Now you've done it!" We parents tend to throw "punch lines" like that into talks with our kids. It helps absolve ourselves of responsibility for their bad or irresponsible behavior. But God is bigger than that. He knew Adam and Eve felt bad about the mess they had made. That's why they hid themselves from each other and from God. They needed to hear words of comfort and hope.

## GROUP DISCUSSION

1. What are some additional "punch lines" parents sometimes inject into conversations with children who have failed?

2. Why do such "punch lines" roll so quickly from our lips?

3. Why didn't God end the "human freewill" experiment that day?

4. What did God and humanity stand to gain by continuing the experiment?

5. Why is it a natural human reaction to hide when we fail?

Before the conversation ended between God and the couple, our loving Heavenly Father offered them both comfort and hope—and He offered them something more: forgiveness and restoration. He showed them a way back to His will and His heart. It wouldn't be an easy way for Him or for them. But He loved them too much to give up on them. He would win them back even if it eventually broke His heart—which it did the day His Son, Jesus, died on the Cross.

## PERSONAL REFLECTION

1. Do you ever feel as if you've messed things up as badly as Adam and Eve did that day?

2. Can you picture God sitting down with you, in the middle of the mess you've made, and helping you figure a way out?

3. How does that make you feel about how much He loves you?

4. Can you grasp new hope for your life as you accept His offer?

Read Gen. 3:14-15 again. Bible scholars tell us that this is the first mention of the gospel message. God offers gospel, or "good news," in His first conversation with the couple following their failure. Notice the couple failed and received judgment for their actions, but the serpent and the ground received the curse. Our loving Heavenly Father spared His children as much grief as He could. However, the consequences of their failure spilled over onto others. The consequences of sin always affect more than simply those who commit the acts.

The animosity between the serpent and the woman may speak of the natural fear most people have of snakes, or it may refer to the perpetual conflict between the tempter and humanity. The reference to "seed" or "offspring" contains a veiled promise of Christ's coming to reverse the effects of the Garden fall. Jesus Christ, the highest and best "Seed" of Eve, would someday come to destroy the spiritual damage sustained that day.

The head-and-heel reference means the tempter will attack Jesus in a nonessential spot (heel), and the wound will not be fatal. Jesus will die on the Cross, but He will rise again. Jesus, on the other hand, will attack the tempter with a bold, daring strike in a vital location (head), and that blow will be fatal. The tempter will be spiritually destroyed and his power over humanity broken.

### GROUP QUESTIONS

1. Why did God comfort the fallen couple so quickly in His first conversation with them following their failure?

2. What consequences of someone else's sins have spilled over into your life?

3. On the very day of the Garden fall, God announced that evil would ultimately be defeated and good would ultimately triumph. What hope for our world or your particular situation do you gain from this realization?

Do you think that before He gave them free will, our Heavenly Father preplanned a provision for humanity's redemption in the event that they disobeyed His command? In other words, did God anticipate the misuse of free will and plan for a way back to His heart? (Rev. 13:8).

We're not sure if the judgments pronounced in Gen. 3:16-19 were ordered by God as a punishment or if He announced the natural consequences of breaking the order that He established. If God ordered the judgments, then He inflicted the pain and toil on us as punishment. If He announced the natural consequences of our actions, then we brought the trouble on ourselves. Childbearing is painful well beyond the day of birth. Parental stress on body, mind, and soul can at times be overwhelming in raising children as God would have us raise them. In the case of the cursed ground, perhaps God did not frustrate agricultural production worldwide but rather announced to Adam that once he left the comforts of Eden he would come face to face with the harsh realities of providing for himself out in an untamed environment. Adam traded the luscious fruit of paradise for the herbs of the field, the food of the pampered for the forage of animals.

If these two possibilities exist, God's words to Adam and Eve went something like this: "You have decided you would rather define your own standards than accept what I provided for you. I will grant you your wish. However, Eve, your children will rebel in this same way against you in demanding their own way. In so doing, they will painfully break your heart just as you have broken Mine. Adam, your desire to have things your way means you will have to establish your new home in a rather hostile environment."

Forfeiting death's immunity turned out to be a blessing in disguise. Once the couple exited Eden, they didn't want to live forever in the hostile, natural world with all its pain and toil, especially without God's immediate presence. They invited death since it brought an end to their path of hardship.

We can't be sure just how those judgments came to us from God, whether decreed or announced as natural consequences. However, we're sure the same effects accrue to us today. If we choose to ignore God's established boundaries and sow our wild oats to the wind, our lives will reap the whirlwind harvest of pain, alienation, sweat, stress, and toil. A life of sin is a hard life, and it ages patrons quickly. Sin's consequences are often built right into the act itself. Take recreational drugs—harm your body. Cheat on your mate—destroy your home. Betray a friend—shatter a relationship. The list is almost endless. Ultimately, if we choose to go sin's way, we'll earn a paycheck we would rather not cash. God knew that and warned us; we choose to ignore His warnings. Carnal knowledge once learned is not easily unlearned. Neither are its consequential effects on us.

## GROUP ACTIVITY

Give each class member four Post-it notes. Have them write their answers to each of the following questions on each of the four notes. Write the numbers 1 through 4 on a chalkboard or dry-erase board. Have class members post their answers under each number. The group leader should read all responses aloud to the entire group.

1. How is Adam and Eve's story every man and every woman's story?

2. Has the tempter's appeals changed much in all of human history?

3. Why do these appeals still work so well up to this very day?

4. Why do people choose to sin in spite of divine warnings and ample examples of others who have taken such doomed paths?

## For Further Study

Heb. 2:14

1 John 3:8

Rom. 7:11

Heb. 3:13

## Further Questions

Take a moment at the conclusion of the session to encourage class participants to place their unanswered questions on note cards, along with this session number. They should then place their cards in an "odds and ends" box provided by the Bible study leader. Attention will be given to these questions in the last session of this study.

# Abraham: The Blameless Man

**Gen. 12:1-3; 17:1-6**

The Bible moves quickly from Adam and Eve's departure from Eden to trouble with their children. Cain murdered Abel, thus proving that rebellion against God passed to Adam and Eve's offspring. From the first family, the Bible then moves quickly in Gen. 5—9 to the spread of human rebellion across the entire population. Scripture tells us in Gen. 6:5-6 that wickedness became pervasive to the point that God was grieved that He had created humanity in the first place. He thus sent a flood to clear the earth of human wickedness and give humanity a fresh start with Noah and his family. Humanity repopulated the earth following the flood, and civilization spread again.

The Bible focuses our attention on one man and his family beginning with Gen. 12. God gives the life of Abraham as an example of one who followed and pleased Him. To this very day Abraham's life shines as a beacon light of direction for us to live a life that pleases God. In Isa. 41:8 God calls Abraham "my friend." That's an outstanding compliment coming from God. Abraham is the only Bible character to receive that description.

## GROUP ACTIVITY

Take two sheets of paper and type one of the following questions on each. Divide the class into two groups. Pass a sheet around each group. Have each person write a response to the question on the paper. The class leader should read all responses once everyone has responded.

1. Put yourself in God's shoes. How do you feel when you see your parental hopes and dreams crumble in the face of human sin and rebellion as described in Gen. 4—6?


2. Would you have given humanity a second chance as God did with Noah, or would you have given up on the human experiment once sin became pervasive as stated in Gen. 6:5-6?


## READ GEN. 12:1-3

Abraham and his extended family first lived in Ur, a very large city on the southeastern side of the Arabian Desert near the Persian Gulf. Idolatry consumed the city, making the worshipers of God feel out of place. So Terah, Abraham's father, moved his family far north to the city of Haran, where they lived until Terah died. God then gave Abraham a plan to move to a new land. He promised to bless Abraham, to make him into a great nation, and to bless those who blessed him.

Why did God select Abraham for this special assignment and blessing? The Bible doesn't indicate any unique qualities to give Abraham an advantage over everyone else on the earth. God's special blessing on Abraham reminds us of His grace. He simply chose to do something special for Abraham and his offspring. It appears that Abraham's only unique quality was his simple faith to live for and trust God. Rom. 4:3 says, "Abraham believed God, and it was credited to him as righteousness."

## GROUP DISCUSSION

1. What does the word "grace" mean to you?

2. In what ways have you received grace in your life?

3. How hard would it be for you to trust God like Abraham if you have no other examples to follow and no support group to assist you?

4. How do you develop simple faith to trust God regardless of the circumstances of life?

5. How does faith in God lead to righteousness?

As you read the life history of Abraham in the Book of Genesis, note how he
- gave up everything to follow God's call;
- moved first to Haran;
- then moved again toward God's land of promise;
- waited patiently for God to give him the land of promise;
- made mistakes;
- endured hardships;
- waited patiently for God to give him a son;
- experienced trials and tests;
- waited patiently for God's spiritual blessing on him and his family.

## GROUP DISCUSSION

1. What impresses you most about the life of Abraham?

2. What surprises you most about his life?

3. How did Abraham develop the patience to trust in God and wait on the fulfillment of His promises when they were delayed so long?

## READ GEN. 17:1-6

God established a contract with Abraham in Gen. 12:2-3 and in Gen. 17:1-6. Imagine that—God sitting down and binding himself contractually to a man and his family! But He did. He promised Abraham all sorts of blessings. Most of these blessings came to reality after Abraham died, but that didn't matter to him. His confidence was in God himself, not in the blessings.

Gen. 17:1 contains God's call to Abraham, and that's particularly interesting in the study of holiness. God said to Abraham, "Walk before me and be blameless." Blameless—that's a powerful notion. The word is used frequently by Paul in his New Testament letters. Check out Paul's usage in Phil. 2:15; Col. 1:22; 1 Thess. 3:13; and 1 Thess. 5:23.

"Blameless" does not imply "perfect," as in free from mistakes. It pictures a person wholeheartedly seeking to do God's will. There's no mix of wanting God's will along with one's own will. It's an undiluted desire to do what God wants one to do. God finds such unmixed desire acceptable and characterizes such a life as blameless. Blamelessness is one of the key biblical manifestations of holiness in the human heart.

Abraham had certainly made his share of mistakes by this point in the story. He lied to the Egyptian Pharaoh (Gen. 12:19) about Sarah being his wife. He and Sarah frustrated God's plan for a child by having Hagar serve as a surrogate mother (Gen. 16:3). But through his occasional errors in judgment, Abraham sought wholeheartedly to find and do God's will. When he stumbled, he sought God's guidance, got back up, and started again.

## PERSONAL REFLECTION

1. What thoughts come to mind when you hear the word "blameless"?

2. Does blamelessness seem like a realistic human goal?

3. Is this something to which you aspire?

4. Would God call Abraham (or us) to a standard that is unattainable?

5. What's the difference between perfect performance and an undiluted desire to do God's will?

Abraham wasn't just one man who exercised faith in God. He became the father of the Hebrew nation, a nation and a race of people who exist to this very day. He also became the father of those who trust and have faith in God. We are members of that family. God calls to us as well, "Walk before me and be blameless."

## FOR FURTHER STUDY

Gen. 22:2-13

1 Kings 2:4

Deut. 18:13

## FURTHER QUESTIONS

Take a moment at the conclusion of the session to encourage class participants to place their unanswered questions on note cards, along with this session number. They should then place their cards in an "odds and ends" box provided by the Bible study leader. Attention will be given to these questions in the last session of this study.

# A Systems Approach

**Exod. 19:16-19; Lev. 1:1—7:34**

Rituals add meaning to our lives. We have rituals in our homes, at church, and at work. For example, at our house everyone gathers at the dinner table at 5:30 each evening. We pray together and then eat our meal and talk about our day together as a family. We have cake and balloons on special occasions. We baptize new converts at church, take communion together monthly, and gather in the fellowship hall for punch and cookies whenever new members join our congregation. We wear clothes with our school colors proudly displayed during homecoming festivities, and our students who play sports wear their Sunday-best clothes on game days. Rituals speak volumes regarding what we believe and what's important to us.

## PERSONAL REFLECTION

1. What are some of your home rituals? Why do you observe them?

2. What are some of your church rituals? What do they say to you?

3. What are some of your work rituals? What do they mean?

We've clearly established in this series of Bible studies that God's purpose in giving us His word is to show us the way to forgiveness for our sins and to restore daily fellowship with Him. Abraham's life offered a crystal-clear example of the fellowship God had in mind for all His children. Abraham wasn't the exception; he was to be the norm, as God hoped it could be. That's why God blessed Abraham's descendents and formed them into a great nation.

Abraham's family settled in the Promised Land. Famine pushed Jacob, his grandson, and his family into Egypt. Four hundred years later, God delivered Abraham's descendents from their Egyptian side trip and brought them back to the Promised Land. God used Moses to bring them back home. Somewhere in all of the family transitions from one generation to the next, folks lost sight of the original plan God had with Abraham.

So God gave Moses a systems approach to the religion of the Hebrew people. He hoped the rituals would be object lessons to speak spiritual truths. He hoped as His people participated in the rituals, they would see past the actions of what they were doing to the fellowship God had with Abraham during his lifetime.

## GROUP DISCUSSION

1. Is it easy for us to get sidetracked from our original intentions, just as the Hebrew people got sidetracked during their years of wandering?


2. As the faith transitions from one generation to the next, why is it easy for essentials to get lost or forgotten?

3. How do we guard or prevent this loss of faith in times of transition?



4. Can ritual help us recall important spiritual truths just as it did for the Hebrew people?



The systems approach God gave Moses for his people is known as the Old Testament sacrificial system. God outlined the procedures for the rituals in the Book of Leviticus. Our biblical passage for this week highlights much of this material. Granted, it sounds foreign to our ears and our life experience. We live too far from the culture and the mind of the ancient Middle East for us to be on familiar territory. However, with a little effort, a look at this material unlocks a goldmine of meaning for our understanding of holiness. In fact, the Book of Leviticus is called "The Book of Holiness." If we grasp even a small portion of the insight hidden in these rituals, we'll have sharper eyes to see what God hopes for us in our relationship with Him.

The plan calls on us to look at each offering prescribed in this passage. Notice the type of ritual, the elements to be used, if it was voluntary or mandatory, and the purpose of the offering. Bear in mind, God was never interested in these rituals for performance's sake. For Him, the goal was always the motive and intention of worshipers' hearts. These rituals purposed to show visually the way folks felt about God.

### The Burnt Offering
### Read Lev. 1:1-17; 6:8-13. (Also see 8:18-21; 16:24.)

The burnt offering was a voluntary offering that atoned for general unintentional sin or the tendency to sin. The offering called for a male animal without defect. Worshipers could offer a bull, ram, or male bird depending on their level of income. As in all blood sacrifices, worshipers laid their hands on the head of the animal and prayed for their guilt to be transferred to the animal. When the animal was slaughtered, the blood was sprinkled on the altar. This act symbolized the seriousness and destructive power of sin.

## The Grain Offering
### Read Lev. 2:1-16; 6:14-23

The grain offering was a voluntary offering given in recognition of God's generous provisions for the worshiper. It called for grain, flour, olive oil, incense, baked bread, and salt. No yeast or honey could be used. It symbolized devotion to God.

## The Fellowship Offering
### Read Lev. 3:1-17; 7:11-34

The fellowship offering was another voluntary offering, made in thanks to God and providing a time of fellowship with Him. The offering accompanied a communal meal with other worshipers. Any animal without defect could be used, along with a variety of breads.

## The Sin Offering
### Read Lev. 4:1—5:13; 6:24-30 (See also 8:14-17; 16:3-22)

The sin offering was mandatory and followed specific unintentional sinning. Intentional sinners found no ritual in this sacrificial system. These sins usually brought exile or death to the sinner. A bull, male goat, female goat, female lamb, dove, or pigeon was offered depending on the income level of the worshiper and whether he was a priest, religious leader, or common person. A larger animal was required of priests and religious leaders because they had greater spiritual influence. Thus, their mistakes bore greater consequences. The language of forgiveness is different in this ritual, signifying that God's forgiveness was not automatically built into the ritual. He granted it at His will based on the intention of the worshiper's heart.

## The Guilt Offering
### Read Lev. 5:14—6:7; 7:1-6

The mandatory guilt offering followed either unintentional sin for which restitution could be made or violations of worship rules. An unblemished ram or lamb could be offered. The unique feature of this offering proved the seriousness of the worshiper by repaying the lost or damaged property of another plus 20 percent of its value. This sacrifice was made in full view of everyone, indicating that God willingly forgave every kind of sin for every type of worshiper.

### GROUP DISCUSSION

1. Why do you suppose in the Old Testament sacrificial system God called for the sacrifice of living animals rather than flowers, plants, or rocks?

2. What is the significance of using the blood of the animal in the ritual?

3. What did God require of worshipers' hearts in order for the sacrifice to be effective?

4. Why do you suppose God's forgiveness was not automatically built into some of these offerings?

5. Should restitution still be practiced today when possible?

These rituals followed a prescribed sequence. Worshipers dealt with sin first, either with the sin or guilt offering. Then they committed themselves to God through the burnt or grain offering. Finally, they enjoyed fellowship with God, the priests, and other worshipers as they celebrated the fellowship.

## PERSONAL REFLECTION

What sequence does your personal worship of God usually take?

Notice some of the holiness symbolism in Leviticus. God is portrayed as a holy deity who must be treated as a Being of purity. Worshipers must display reverence, orderliness, respectfulness, and every other virtue of one who honors this holy God. God required that the animals offered for sacrifice must be physically perfect. He was too holy and the ritual too sacred for worshipers to bring bargain-rack rejects to sacrifice. The priests themselves had to be without physical deformity in order to be worthy of offering these sacrifices. No discrimination against the handicapped was intended; this symbol reminded worshipers that God deserved the best in every way. Worshipers could not appear before God with sores, burns, or skin diseases for that same reason. Every detail of the place and manner of the sacrifice receives attention in the Book of Holiness, because complete devotion to God from everyone involved was of utmost importance.

## GROUP ACTIVITY

Give each class member a note card. Have each member respond to the following question on his or her card. Collect all cards and read them aloud to the entire group.

Now that you have reviewed God's systems approach to worshiping Him, what new thing have you learned about holiness from this study?

## For Further Study

Exod. 33:9

Ps. 145:18

Acts 17:24-27

## Further Questions

Take a moment at the conclusion of the session to encourage class participants to place their unanswered questions on note cards, along with this session number. They should then place their cards in an "odds ands ends" box provided by the Bible study leader. Attention will be given to these questions in the last session of this study.

# A Better Approach

**Heb. 10:1-18**

When I was a high school student, I spent every weekday afternoon practicing with the marching band. Frankly, at the time it seemed like slow torture. Now I can see that those practices helped me learn several life skills such as patience, perseverance, discipline, and precision, just to name a few. But back then it didn't seem worthwhile. I can still hear the band director's stern words: "Stop! We're going to do that drill over again. Come on, people—let's try to get it right this time!" So over and over we practiced the same routine until we "got it right."

That's exactly what the writer to the Hebrews had in mind when he wrote this passage of scripture. Day after day and month after month, priests made offering after offering on the altars of the Tabernacle or Temple. Each time an offering rose up to God, worshipers prayed that they would "get it right this time." But they didn't. So the blood flowed in rivers from the altars, and meat went up in flames while worshipers returned home with the same haunting question that brought them there in the first place: "Can I find forgiveness for my sins?"

## PERSONAL REFLECTION

Think of a physical, musical, or mental exercise you practiced over and over for a long period of time until it became second nature.

1. What did you learn from this activity?

2. What was most frustrating about it?


3. What was most rewarding about it?


## READ HEB. 10:1-4

Practicing these offerings did not make the worshipers perfect. In fact, it only mocked their souls' sad cry. The sacrifices failed because they were only shadows or signposts pointing in the direction of the true, final sacrifice of Christ. They offered only a temporary remedy that never gave worshipers a feeling of wholeness or completeness.

Animal sacrifices never solved the deep-seated problem of the human heart. Spiritual needs can't be met by physical rituals alone. So worshipers left the ritual with the sin guilt they had brought with them. The ritual remained outward, not inward. The very fact that the rituals needed to be repeated annually reminded the people of the rituals' tragic flaw. The word used in Heb. 10:3 for "reminder" is found elsewhere in the Bible only in conjunction with the Lord's Supper (Luke 22:19). That's no coincidence. It says in essence, "While animal sacrifices remind us of our sins, the Lord's Supper reminds us that God forgives our sin because of Christ's sacrifice for us."


## GROUP DISCUSSION

Put yourself in the sandals of an Old Testament worshiper. Answer the following questions from that perspective.
1. Does the sacrificial ritual offer you some spiritual benefit and blessing?

2. How does it make you feel to offer sacrifices year after year, without feeling relief from your guilt?

3. Why do you keep doing it year after year? What is your hope in the repetition?

4. If one last sacrifice could be made for you that would solve your problem once and for all, would you be interested?

READ HEB. 10:5-9

Heb. 10:5-9 draws from Ps. 40:6-8 and references four sacrifices: "sacrifice" (referring to the animal sacrifice of the peace offering), "offering" (referring to the grain offering), "burnt offering," and "sin offering." God's true desire for worshipers can't be found in making sacrifices. He wants our obedience to His will.

Verses 8-10 make comments on the passage. The switch from singular references ("sacrifice" and "offering") in verse 5 to plural references ("sacrifices" and "offerings") in verse 8 expresses a lacking in the entire sacrificial system. God's displeasure with ritual for ritual's sake is again emphasized in verse 8. This is not to say that God disapproves of the sacrifices; it's to say He desires our obedience more than our performance of ritual.

## GROUP ACTIVITY

Divide the class into three groups. Assign each group a different question from the list below. Have each group write its responses on three large sheets of poster paper and read them to the entire class.

1. God is obviously not saying He does not want the sacrifices performed that He ordered. What attitude or spirit, then, does God seek in true worshipers?

2. Why do we tend to fall into a patterned routine when we perform an act or ritual again and again?

3. How do you avoid falling into such a patterned routine?

## READ HEB. 10:10

Heb. 10:10 contains one of the most important insights into our holiness to be found in the entire Bible. Verses 7 and 9 speak of God's will. Verse 10 says that by this will of God believers are sanctified or made holy. The writer refers here to God's act of cleansing our hearts from sin and setting us apart for His good pleasure and service. The significance of this verse lies in the connection between Christ's sacrificial death on the Cross and our sanctification. His death made possible our sanctification. We hear often of Christ's death bringing the forgiveness of our sins; we tend not to hear as much about His death purchasing our sanctification.

The tenses of the verbs in this verse and in verse 14 remind us that our sanctification is a once-and-for-all act ("we have been made holy") and an ongoing process ("those who are being made holy"). Christ's sacrifice on the Cross was "once for all." However, His continuing work in our lives goes on for a lifetime.

## PERSONAL REFLECTION

1. How does it make you feel to realize that God willed your sanctification so much that He offered His Son on the Cross to make it possible?

2. In what ways is your sanctification a once-and-for-all act?

3. In what ways is your sanctification an ongoing process?

## READ HEB. 10:11-18

Christ and the priests are contrasted in two significant ways in Heb. 10:11-18. The first contrast involves standing and sitting. It pictures the priests standing as they perform sacrifices over and over while Christ sits, due to the fact that His sacrificial work is complete. The second contrast involves the concepts of "offering" and "having offered." It pictures the priest performing his duties repeatedly while Christ completed His once and for all.

Two insights leap from verse 14, both of which emphasize that our sanctification is God's work. We have already noted the progressive nature of our sanctification as we are "being made holy." Note, too, the passive voice of "those who are being made." Our good works or faithful observance of a prescribed set of regulations fail to accomplish our sanctification. We do not earn it. God gives it to us by His grace because of what Christ has done for us.

Verse 16 offers the key feature of Christ's sacrifice that makes it superior to the Old Testament sacrificial system. The writer quotes Jer. 31:33, in which the prophet saw the day coming when God's Holy Spirit would live within believers. From within their hearts and minds, He would direct them and provide all they would need in order to avoid sin. An internal work outperforms external ritual hands down.

The passage closes with the reminder that while Old Testament worshipers returned home with sin's guilt, Christ has made it possible for our sins to be erased and the debt paid in full. The Old Testament systems approach served a necessary place in salvation history, but Christ's death on the Cross rendered it obsolete and made possible the holiness that God planned for His people when He placed them in the Garden of Eden. Christ's sacrifice on the Cross fulfilled God's promise to Adam and Eve expressed in Gen. 3:15 and put God's plan for His children back on track.

## GROUP DISCUSSION

1. How does it make you feel when you realize that Christ is now sitting at the right hand of God with His sacrificial work for you completed?

2. If sanctification is a gift from God that He freely gives, then what should our response be to Him?

3. In what ways does an internal work of the Holy Spirit in our hearts outperform the external rituals of the sacrificial system?

4. What significance do you attach to the possibility of having your guilt for sin completely removed and knowing for certain that your sins are forgiven?

## FOR FURTHER STUDY

This passage clearly connects Christ's sacrifice on the Cross with our sanctification. Trace this line of thought further in Hebrews with the following passages of scripture:

Heb. 9:14

Heb. 10:14, 29

Heb. 13:12

## FURTHER QUESTIONS

Take a moment at the conclusion of the session to encourage class participants to place their unanswered questions on note cards, along with this session number. They should then place their cards in an "odds and ends" box provided by the Bible study leader. Attention will be given to these questions in the last session of this study.

# Holiness Requires the Cross

**Heb. 13:11-16, 20-21**

I worked as an orderly at a hospital while attending seminary. My boss was a complete germ freak! He insisted that we wash our hands before going into patients' rooms, after we returned from delivering supplies, before we touched certain hospital equipment—pretty much every time we turned around. And we had to use antibacterial soap and hot water. The hospital welcomed nothing unclean.

The Old Testament sacrificial system proposed similar issues in establishing rules for cleanliness in the Tabernacle and the camp of tents occupied by God's people. There was a major difference, though, in the cleanliness protected in the sacrificial system and what was involved in my hospital experience. Ceremonial or ritual cleanliness carried the spiritual significance of maintaining an environment worthy of worship for our holy God.

## PERSONAL REFLECTION

Think of the habits you practice at work or home to promote a clean environment. Name the chemicals, brushes, masks, tools, mops, and other paraphernalia you employ in your efforts. Why do you go to such lengths to promote cleanliness? Now transfer this thought to the spiritual realm, and note how important this concept becomes for our Bible study.

## READ LEV. 4:12; 13:45-46

We've already studied a portion of the background for this week's Bible study. It comes from Lev. 4:12; 13:45-46. Attention in these passages focuses on the land "outside the camp." By that we mean the area in the wilderness, far re-moved from either the Tabernacle or the tent city of God's people. Once God's people returned to the Promised Land and sacrificed animals in the Temple in Jerusalem, the con-cept of "outside the camp" referred to the wasteland outside of Jerusalem's city walls. This symbol reminded the people that God's presence not only filled the Tabernacle and the Temple and the courtyard surrounding these worship centers, but it also pervaded their homes as well.

The symbolism of "outside the camp" offers an important lesson both about our sin and about our God. God is a holy God; sacrifices offered to Him must be offered in a manner that promotes ceremonial purity and shows consideration for the seriousness of sin. God wanted His people to take sin as se-riously as He did. So the worshiper placed the sacrificial animal on the altar, laid his hands on the animal's head, and prayed a prayer to ask God to transfer his sins to the animal. In other words, the worshiper requested that God see the animal as a sinner and himself as innocent. Worshipers exercised faith that God would reverse their spiritual conditions. Once the animal became a sinner in God's eyes, the priest killed it on the altar of sacrifice. Thus, the animal died in place of the worshiper.

Nevertheless, simply killing the "sinner" animal did not complete the ritual process. Even the carcass contained spiri-tual defilement. Proper disposal protected the spiritual purity of the Tabernacle area and the tent city. The priest carried the condemned carcass "outside the camp," burned it, and prop-erly disposed of the ashes, thus symbolizing the removal of sin from God's people.

## GROUP DISCUSSION

1. Why does God offer us rituals as a part of our worship of Him?

2. What does the sacrificing of animals say about God's view of sin?

3. What does His offer to allow animals to take the place of sinners say about God's love and mercy for humanity?

4. What does the ritual of taking the condemned carcass outside the camp say about the way God treats our sins once we confess them to Him?

5. How does His willingness to leave our sins outside the camp encourage us to do the same and walk away from them both in memory and practice?

## READ HEB. 13:11-16

What a powerful symbol! Just as the priest carried the condemned sacrificial animal "outside the camp," so the Roman soldiers carried Jesus outside Jerusalem's walls to hang Him on the Cross. Jesus' death as an outsider on Calvary accomplished in reality for us what the sacrificial animal's death accomplished only symbolically. We studied this thought in our last session—the symbolism of the Old Testament sacrificial system served as a signpost pointing to the real sacrifice God had in mind, a sacrifice possessing the power to truly forgive sin and remove its guilt.

Also, in much the same way as Old Testament worshipers prayed for God to allow the animal to represent them and die for their sins, God allowed His Son, Jesus Christ, to represent us and die in our place on Calvary. We must exercise the same faith the Old Testament worshipers exercised in believing that God would allow them to identify with the animal's death. So we have faith and identify with Christ's death, seeing it as "for us."

## Group Discussion

1. Does this study of the Old Testament sacrificial system cast new light for you on Jesus' death on Calvary?

2. In what ways can you verbalize the way you understand letting Jesus represent you in death for your sins?

3. In what ways can you verbalize the way you identify with Jesus as He died for your sins?

4. What should this identification say about the way we now treat both our past sins and lure to sin again?

5. What role does faith play in all of this?

Verse 13 casts a new light on the way God wants us to identify with His Son. Yes, we identify with Jesus as He died on the Cross for our sins, but that's not all. Now that we're believers and part of God's family, He wants us to identify with Christ by stepping outside the persuasive influence of secular society with its constant invitation to place other gods before Him. We "go with Him outside the camp" by refusing to let the world squeeze us into its mold. As Paul advises us in Rom. 12:2, "Do not conform any longer to the pattern of this world." Materialism, constant activity, sports, music, movies, and a host of other things scream for our time and money. But more importantly, they scream for our minds and our allegiance. Followers of Jesus Christ demonstrate their faith in Him by walking away from the world's lure and taking their stand with Him "outside the camp," where our holy God is honored as the supreme sovereign of our lives.

The mention of an enduring city reminds us that our journey with Christ "outside the camp" will ultimately end in heaven, where we'll live with Him forever. By the way, Scripture often ties the two thoughts of holiness and heaven together as it does in this verse. That must imply a strong connection!

## GROUP ACTIVITY

Divide the class into four groups. Assign each group a different one of the following questions. Have each group report responses to the entire class when ready.

1. In what ways does society attempt to lure us into worshiping other gods?

2. In what ways does the world attempt to squeeze us into thinking and valuing as it does?

3. Name some concrete ways you can take your stand with Jesus Christ "outside the camp."

4. Why do you suppose God often follows His presentations on holiness with presentations on heaven?

## READ HEB. 13:20-21

The closing benediction of Heb. 13:20-21 is packed with symbolism that draws together in one thought the concepts that make Christ's new covenant superior. We're reminded that our God is both the author of peace and the One who brings true peace to our hearts. Christ's blood purchased this new covenant. Christ's resurrection from the dead validated the Father's blessing on His life and the truthfulness of His ministry. Christ is now our great shepherd. He equips and empowers us to do God's will. God works within us to accomplish His purposes. All the praise and glory for what's being accomplished in our lives go to Jesus Christ.

This week's study reminds us of the triple benefit of the Cross. That benefit includes forgiveness of sins, cleansing from sin, and eternal life. God's incredible work in us leads naturally to holiness. Praise His name!

## GROUP DISCUSSION

1. Compare this closing benediction with God's original plan for humanity outlined in the Garden of Eden. In what ways are God's original plans accomplished?

2. What do Jesus' death and resurrection accomplish for us that we can't do for ourselves, according to this passage?

3. What do you suppose "everything good" in verse 21 refers to?

4. How do we realize God's plans and dreams for our lives? Is it more in what we do for Him or in what He does through us?

## FOR FURTHER STUDY

More connections can be made between holiness and the Cross by studying the following passages:

Rom. 3:23-25

Rom. 8:31-39

Eph. 5:25-27

## FURTHER QUESTIONS

Take a moment at the conclusion of the session to encourage class participants to place their unanswered questions on note cards, along with this session number. They should then place their cards in an "odds and ends" box provided by the Bible study leader. Attention will be given to these questions in the last session of this study.

# Tying It All Together

We started this book with the idea that God is holy, and He calls His children to be holy as well. He devised a plan for our holiness that involved deep, personal relationship with Him. The plan didn't work as anticipated, however, because we came up with our own plan. Our plan involved going our own way and doing our own thing rather than following God's prescription for our lives. God gave us the freedom to choose for ourselves; we used that freedom to choose not to follow Him. That choice changed our lives forever and brought unwelcome consequences to our world.

Our study of holiness in Book 1 deals primarily with God's plan for humanity and the many ways He worked to get His plan back on track. We want to take time now to review what we've already studied and to answer questions that students may have. We'll begin this week's study with a group discussion to address those unanswered questions.

## GROUP ACTIVITY

Bible study participants have been encouraged throughout this study to write their unanswered questions on note cards and to place the cards in the "odds and ends" box. Use time at the beginning of this session to address these questions in the form of a group discussion. The Bible study leader should add clarity wherever necessary and draw each question, with answers, to a close. It's possible that more time will be needed to adequately address lingering questions than one study session can accommodate. In that case, plan ahead to make this study a two-part session. It's important that you address all the issues that are raised before moving on to a final wrap-up of the study material.

## READ GEN. 3:14-15

God easily could have walked away from the "humanity project" that day. He could have labeled it a failure and given up on us. He could have wiped the slate clean and started all over with another set of characters. But for reasons known only to Him, He didn't. He linked himself to this project for the long haul. Rather than giving up on us, He determined to find a way to restore His relationship with us and bring us back to himself. The first three chapters of Genesis recount this part of the story. This particular passage shows God involving himself directly in talking to Adam and Eve about a restoration plan. The rest of the Old Testament unfolds the step-by-step process God used to bring us to a point of recognizing our need for Him and pointing us to His remedy for our spiritual problem.

## GROUP DISCUSSION

No one knows for sure, but why do you think God didn't give up on us when we rebelled against Him but rather devised a plan to bring us back to himself?

## READ GEN. 17:1-2

Abraham receives attention throughout the Bible as a man who pleased God. His performance wasn't always perfect; the Bible recounts several of his big mistakes. However, God never asked him for perfect performance. He called him to be blameless. There's a big difference between "blameless" and "flawless." "Blameless" implies that we wholeheartedly seek God's will. Our desire yields to His desire. From that perspective, Abraham pleased God. In fact, God called him "my friend" in Isa. 41:8. Now that's a compliment when you consider the source—the Creator of the universe!

## GROUP DISCUSSION

1. Look over Abraham's life. What was it about the spirit and nature of his heart that pleased God so much?

2. Can you imitate Abraham's example in your own life? Why or why not?

## READ EXOD. 19:16-19

Exod. 19:16-19 reminds us that God initiated a plan to restore humanity to relationship with himself. He signaled a meeting with the Hebrew people with an all-out light-and-sound show. Everyone who saw it stood in awe. Truthfully, it scared them nearly to death. No one doubted that God Almighty commanded thunder and lightning to announce this meeting. Moses agreed to represent the Hebrew people before God. At this meeting, God gave Moses an entire system of religious rituals for restoring a right standing between the Hebrew people and their Maker. We call it the Old Testament sacrificial system.

## GROUP DISCUSSION

1. Why did God give the Hebrew people such a hands-on set of rituals for their worship practices?

2. Why did God make these worship practices so symbolic?

3. What are the big lessons you learn about the plan of salvation from the Old Testament sacrificial system?

### READ HEB. 10:1-4

New Testament writers looked back on the Old Testament sacrificial system and critiqued the problems with it. It remained flawed through the many years of usage. The sacrificial system contained several problems, the biggest being that it didn't remove worshipers' guilt. They left the offering of their sacrifices wondering if God accepted them and forgave their sins. They kept coming back year after year, and they kept offering more sacrifices. It's all they knew to do.

### GROUP DISCUSSION

Compare your understanding of God's plan of salvation through the new covenant of Jesus Christ with what an Old Testament believer understood through the Old Testament sacrificial system.

1. How are the two covenants alike?

2. How are they different?

3. Which is superior and why?

The Old Testament prophets occasionally received unusual insights into God's promised new covenant as they looked ahead to God's new future for humanity. Their visions weren't very comprehensive—just bits and pieces of information across the centuries. But these brief insights gave God's people something to look forward to. The prophets knew the new covenant would not occur in their lifetimes, but they had confidence to trust God to bring it to pass just as He promised. Isaiah, Jeremiah, Ezekiel, and Joel received insightful glimpses of this new covenant. As so many people say, hindsight is 20/20. We look back on these prophecies and see the powerful truth contained in them. They make much more sense to us than they did to the Old Testament prophets.

## GROUP ACTIVITY

Divide the Bible study group into four groups. Have each one read the following passages of scripture and answer the questions below.

Isa. 44:3

Jer. 31:31-33

Ezek. 36:23, 25-27

Joel 2:28-29

1. Summarize the main point of the prophet's message.


2. What did the prophet see coming in the new covenant?


3. What symbols did the prophet use to describe God's new plan?

4. What did the prophet see as the improvement of the new covenant over the old?

## FINAL GROUP ACTIVITY

Break the class into pairs. Have each pair share its responses to each of the following questions. Then have one member of each pair share the high points of their discussion with the entire group.

1. What has been your greatest insight about God's plan for humanity from this Bible study?

2. What has been the hardest concept for you to grasp in this Bible study?

3. What is your favorite passage of scripture from this Bible study?

4. How has your life changed as a result of this Bible study?

## MOVING ON

Our adventure with God doesn't stop with understanding God's plan, which we've discussed in this Bible study series. Yes, humanity fouled up God's original plan, but God found a way to put that plan back in place. Throughout the Old Testament we read bits and pieces here and there about how God will eventually institute a new covenant with humanity. This new covenant will personalize the plan in ways that the Old Testament prophets only dreamed possible. In the next book of this Bible study series we will consider our adventure with God from the perspective of "The Journey Within," or a look at *personal* holiness. In Book 2 we'll learn how God cares for every detail in providing the means for us to experience a relationship with Him that can be described only as a big adventure. Words fail to adequately describe the thrill of partnering with God on the holiness road. Join us as we continue our exploration of God's amazing journey with His children.